BLACKFOOT

Big Buddy Books
An Imprint of Abdo Publishing
www.abdopublishing.com

Sarah Tieck

www.abdopublishing.com

Published by Abdo Publishing, a division of ABDO, PO Box 398166, Minneapolis, Minnesota 55439.
Copyright © 2015 by Abdo Consulting Group, Inc. International copyrights reserved in all countries. No part
of this book may be reproduced in any form without written permission from the publisher. Big Buddy Books™
is a trademark and logo of Abdo Publishing.

Printed in the United States of America, North Mankato, Minnesota.
102014
012015

THIS BOOK CONTAINS
RECYCLED MATERIALS

Cover Photo: *Getty Images*: Eye Ubiquitous/Contributor; Shutterstock.com.
Interior Photos: © Eye Ubiquitous/Alamy (p. 19); *Getty Images*: Werner Forman/Contributor (p. 27);
    Glowimages.com (pp. 16, 17); © iStockphoto.com (pp. 11, 21, 26); Library of Congress (p. 13);
    © David Muenker/Alamy (pp. 5, 29); © National Geographic Image Collection/Alamy (pp. 9, 15, 25);
    Wikpedia.com (pp. 23, 30).

Coordinating Series Editor: Rochelle Baltzer
Contributing Editors: Megan M. Gunderson, Marcia Zappa
Graphic Design: Adam Craven

Library of Congress Cataloging-in-Publication Data

Tieck, Sarah, 1976-
  Blackfoot / Sarah Tieck.
    pages cm. -- (Native Americans)
  Audience: Ages 7-11.
  ISBN 978-1-62403-577-7
1. Siksika Indians--Juvenile literature. I. Title.
  E99.S54T54 2015
  978.004'97352--dc23
                          2014029812

CONTENTS

Amazing People

Hundreds of years ago, North America was mostly wild, open land. Native American tribes lived on the land. They had their own languages and **customs**.

The Blackfoot are one Native American tribe. They are known for their Sun Dance and fighting skills. Let's learn more about these Native Americans.

Did You Know?

The Blackfoot were named for the dark-colored bottoms of their moccasins.

4

The Blackfoot decorated their clothes with patterns and feathers. Today, they wear traditional clothing for special events.

BLACKFOOT TERRITORY

Blackfoot homelands were in what is now Montana, Idaho, and Wyoming. The people also lived in Canada in Alberta, Saskatchewan, and British Columbia. Several different groups are part of the Blackfoot Nation. These include the Piegan, the Blood, and the Siksika.

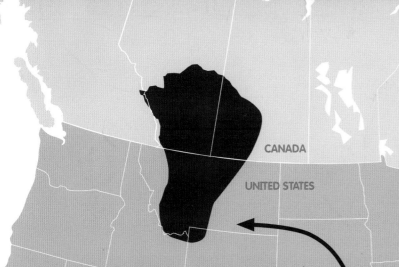

BLACKFOOT HOMELANDS

CANADA

BRITISH
COLUMBIA

ALBERTA

SASKATCHEWAN

MONTANA

IDAHO

UNITED STATES

WYOMING

N
W E
S

CANADA

UNITED STATES

HOME LIFE

Blackfoot families lived in teepees. A teepee had a frame made of wooden poles. It was covered with animal skins. Since the tribes moved often, a teepee was easy to set up and take down.

The women of the tribe carried and built the teepees.

9

What They Ate

The Blackfoot were skilled hunters. They mostly hunted buffalo, deer, antelope, and elk. They also gathered food from the land. They ate berries and other plants, such as camas bulbs or roots.

Buffalo (*left*) and elk (*right*) were major food sources. Meat was boiled, roasted, and dried. It was also made into stew and sausage.

DAILY LIFE

The Blackfoot lived in bands. These included 50 to 100 people. Bands were led by one or more chiefs. They moved with the buffalo and at the change of seasons.

The Blackfoot made clothing from animal fur and hides. They wore moccasins. Women wore dresses. Men had leggings, shirts, and cloths to cover their lower bodies.

The Blackfoot followed buffalo, which they relied on for food and clothing.

A typical Blackfoot family might include two men, three women, and three children.

In a Blackfoot band, people had different jobs. Men were warriors, hunters, or chiefs.

Women took care of the children and ran the homes. They gathered food and prepared meat and hides.

Children learned by helping and watching others in the community. Men taught the boys and women taught the girls.

Most hunters and warriors were men. But sometimes, women joined the men on a hunt or in battle.

15

Made by Hand

The Blackfoot made many objects by hand. They often used natural materials. These arts and crafts added beauty to everyday life.

War Clothing

The Blackfoot wore special clothing for battle. War clothing was decorated with porcupine quills, beads, and fringes. This showed status.

Headddresses

 Blackfoot men wore headdresses in battle. These were similar to hats. Some had bison horns, feathers, beads, and fur.

Embroidery

The Blackfoot were talented at sewing. They sewed designs into their clothes. This is called embroidery. The Blackfoot often used beads and porcupine quills in their designs.

Spirit Life

The Blackfoot believed animals and natural elements had power. They observed **ceremonies**, **rituals**, and other practices throughout the year. They believed these helped keep them safe.

Today, the Sun Dance remains an important Blackfoot ceremony. It is held in late spring or early summer. The people gather for eight days for dancing, singing, praying, and other activities.

Dancing is a part of ceremonies and other activities.

STORYTELLERS

Long ago, the Blackfoot painted pictographs on <u>buffalo</u> hides and carved petroglyphs in stone. These pictures told stories. Today, storytellers share stories to pass on **culture** and history.

Some Blackfoot stories are about how the world and people came to be. Others describe famous battles. Napi, or Old Man, is an important character in many stories.

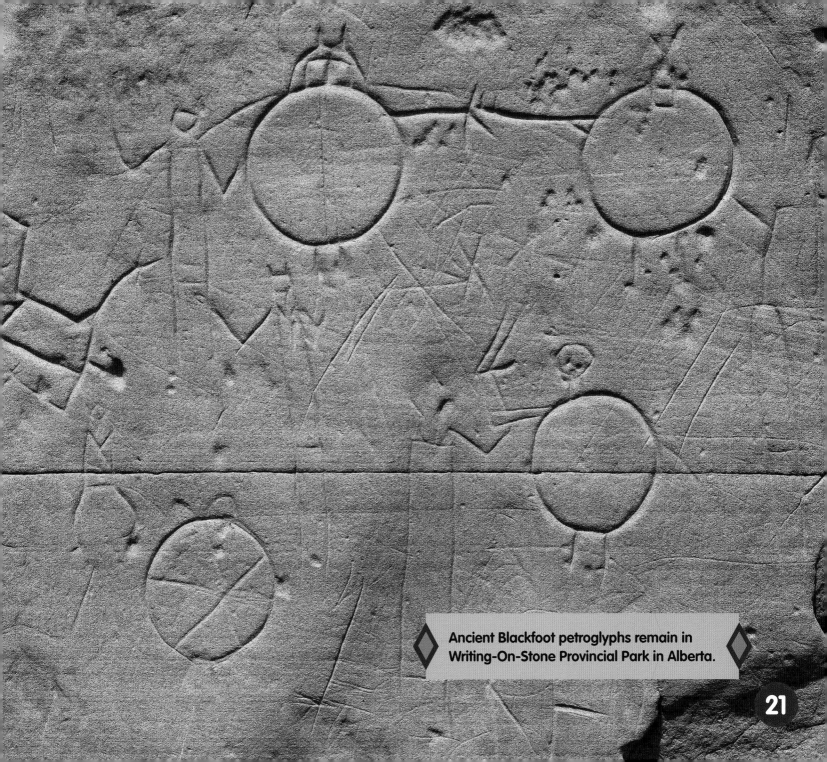

Ancient Blackfoot petroglyphs remain in Writing-On-Stone Provincial Park in Alberta.

FIGHTING FOR LAND

The first Blackfoot lived in wooded areas. Before Europeans arrived, the people used dogs to move to open, grassy **plains**. By 1750, they had horses. They began expanding their territory.

In 1831, an American fur trading company set up Fort Piegan by the Missouri River. They wanted to trade with the Blackfoot.

Horses changed many parts of Blackfoot life.

Over time, the Blackfoot began to trade goods with settlers. But, they got **smallpox** from them. And, settlers killed more buffalo than they needed. The Blackfoot could not get enough food. Many people died.

In 1855, the US government set aside land for the Blackfoot. It later became a **reservation**. The Blackfoot began farming and **ranching**. Today, they welcome visitors to their lands in the United States and Canada.

Did You Know?

Today, there are about 27,000 Blackfoot in the United States. About 15,000 live in Canada.

The Blackfoot often brought their furs to trading posts.

25

BACK IN TIME

About 1730

The Blackfoot saw horses for the first time. By 1750, they had their own. Before this, they hunted on foot.

After 1750

The Blackfoot took over much surrounding land. They had a large area of the plains in what is now Canada and the American West.

1851

The Treaty of Fort Laramie established the boundaries of Blackfoot territory in the United States.

1934

After many years of being against the law, the Sun Dance became legal again.

1877

The Canadian government set aside land for the Blackfoot in Alberta.

1994

Pikuni was chosen as the official language of the Blackfoot Council.

The Blackfoot Today

The Blackfoot have a long, rich history. They are remembered for their buffalo hunts and religious beliefs.

Blackfoot roots run deep. Today, the people have kept alive those special things that make them Blackfoot. Even though times have changed, many people carry the **traditions**, stories, and memories of the past into the present.

Today, the Blackfoot talk to kids about what life was like for their ancestors.

"What is life? It is the flash of a firefly in the night. It is the breath of a buffalo in the wintertime. It is the little shadow, which runs across the grass and loses itself in the sunset."

— Chief Crowfoot

GLOSSARY

ceremony a formal event on a special occasion.

culture (KUHL-chuhr) the arts, beliefs, and ways of life of a group of people.

custom a practice that has been around a long time and is common to a group or a place.

plains flat or rolling land without trees.

ranch to live or work on a large farm where people raise cattle, horses, or sheep.

reservation (reh-zuhr-VAY-shuhn) a piece of land set aside by the government for Native Americans to live on.

ritual (RIH-chuh-wuhl) a formal act or set of acts that is repeated.

smallpox a sickness that causes fever, skin marks, and often death.

tradition (truh-DIH-shuhn) a belief, a custom, or a story handed down from older people to younger people.

WEBSITES

To learn more about Native Americans, visit **booklinks.abdopublishing.com**. These links are routinely monitored and updated to provide the most current information available.

INDEX